ENGLISH MADE EASILY

Workbook in English 6

by

EMILIANA EBORA PANAMBO

COPYRIGHT @ 2023 ENGLISH MADE EASILY
By Emiliana Ebora Panambo

ISBN:
Hardbound-978-621-470-575-7
MOBI/KINDLE-978-621-470-576-4
Softbound/Paperback-978-621-470-577-1

Published by:
Poetry Planet Book Publishing House
Rosario, Pozorrubio, Pangasinan, Philippines
Contact Number: 09554960094
Email: maritesritumalta@gmail.com

ACKNOWLEDGMENT

The author is indebted to the following who shared expertise and assistance in making this book conceptually and thematically equipped.

- To the Almighty Father who blessed me with knowledge and wisdom.

- To the able and enduring members and staff in this publishing house.

- To my Tatay Ricardo D. Ebora and Inay Erlinda M. Ebora.

- To my husband Eric B. Panambo.

- To my children Patricia Erica E. Panambo and Lucas Emerson E. Panambo who served as inspiration in making this book.

- To the authors and publishers of the books which were used as references.

- My profound gratitude to all of you.

The Author

DEDICATION

Thank you, my dear family,
my kids;
brother and sisters;
and my nieces
for constantly inspiring me
to be the best that I can be.
You are my total package
of hope and love from God.

TABLE OF CONTENTS

Quarter 1

Quarter 2

Quarter 3

1st QUARTER

LESSON 1

Regular Plural Nouns

Plural nouns indicate that there is more than one object or subject being discussed.

Regular nouns do not change their spellings during pluralization. They become plural when you add–s or –es.

The vowel or consonant before the last letter of singular nouns also dictates the correct plural of regular nouns.

Regular singular nouns follow these standard rules to become plural nouns:

Rule: 1

- Adding-**s** to the singular nouns.

book – books	chair– chairs
page – pages	computer-computers

Rule: 2

- Adding-**es** if the singular noun ends in **ch**, **sh**, **s**, **ss**, **x**, and **z**.

bus – buses	bench – benches
box – boxes	brush – brushes
truss- trusses	buzz- buzzes

- Some singular nouns that end in **s** or **z** requires doubling the s or z and adding **–es**.

> gas – gasses   fez - fezzes

Rule #3

- Adding -**s** to nouns ending in **o** and preceded by a **vowel**.

> studio – studios   portfolio – portfolios
>
> radio – radios   cameo – cameos

- Adding **-s** or **-es** to nouns ending in **o** and preceded by a **consonant**.

> piano – pianos   avocado – avocados
>
> volcano – volcano/volcanoes   potato – potato/potatoes

Rule #4

- Changing **y** to **i** of singular nouns preceded by a **consonant** and adding **-es**.

> lady – ladies   country – countries
>
> supply – supplies   duty – duties

- For singular nouns with a **vowel** before **y**, just add **–s** to make them plural.

<table>
<tr><td>monkey – monkeys</td><td>ray – rays</td></tr>
<tr><td>day – days</td><td>toy – toys</td></tr>
</table>

Rule #5

- Changing **f** or **fe** to **ves**.

<table>
<tr><td>wife – wives</td><td>loaf – loaves</td></tr>
<tr><td>wolf – wolves</td><td>life - lives</td></tr>
</table>

- Exceptions: The following regular nouns form their plurals by adding **s**.

<table>
<tr><td>grief – griefs</td><td>roof– roofs</td></tr>
<tr><td>chief – chiefs</td><td>belief – beliefs</td></tr>
</table>

ACTIVITIES

Activity 1: Write the plural forms of the following regular nouns.

1. thief - ___________
2. tax   - ___________
3. city - ___________
4. photo - ___________
5. tomato - ___________

6. chimney - ___________
7. echo - ___________
8. dress - ___________
9. lady - ___________
10. star - ___________

Activity 2: Identify whether the following nouns are plural or singular.

___________ 1. valley

___________ 2. mosquitoes

___________ 3. bush

___________ 4. crayons

___________ 5. mementos

___________ 6. cherries

___________ 7. mugs

___________ 8. country

___________ 9. gulfs

___________ 10. coal

Activity 3: Complete the following sentences by choosing the right plural of the nouns.

1. We have many ___________ (book, books) at home.

2. Do you know the ___________ (persons, person) who sang last night?

3. He broke the only ___________ (vases, vase) in the living room.

4. Many (countries, country) ___________ are waiting for the vaccines.

5. I have two (sister, sisters) ___________ and one (brothers, brother) ___________ .

6. The bird (fly, flies) _______________ up high.

7. My (family, families) _______________ will celebrate Christmas at home.

8. His (wives, wife) _______________ is very beautiful.

9. The (girls, girl) _______________ in red dress is my cousin.

10.   I need two (boy, boys) _______________ as volunteers.

Activity 4: Find the plural nouns and use them in sentences.

city	tomato	wishes	bedrooms	glass
kisses	churches	dog	sky	theories

1. ____

2. ____

3. ____

4. ____

5. ____

LESSON 2

Irregular Plural Nouns

Irregular nouns do not follow the standard rules in pluralization. They do not change at all or change completely.

A. Irregular nouns form their plural by changing the vowels **–an** to **–en** or **–oo** to **–ee**.

tooth – teeth	foot – feet
man-men	woman – women

B. Irregular nouns **change their spelling** substantially during pluralization.

mouse – mice	person- people
child -children	louse – lice

C. Irregular nouns that **do not change** their spelling when made plural.

series	sheep	measles	trousers
species	scissors	mumps	cattle

D. Irregular nouns that are derived from Green or Latin use the plural endings from these languages.

- Those ending in **–us** form their plural by changing **us** to **i.** Anglicized versions are also formed by adding **es**.

fungus -fungi   cactus –cacti

nucleus – nuclei   alumnus –alumni

cactus –cacti

  focus – foci or focuses nucleus – nuclei

 radius – radii or radiuses

E. Irregular nouns ending in **–is** form their plural changing **is** to **es**.

cactus –cacti

axis – axes   crisis - crises

        nucleus – nuclei

thesis – theses   analysis - analyses

F. Irregular nouns ending in **–on** form their plural changing **on** to **a**.

cactus –cacti

 phenomenon – phenomena

       nucleus – nuclei

 criterion   – criteria

G. Irregular nouns ending in –**um** form their plural by changing **um** to **a**.

> cactus –cacti
>   curriculum – curricula   bacterium - bacteria
>   nucleus – nuclei
>   memorandum-memoranda   datum - data

H. Irregular nouns ending in –**x** form their plural by adding–**es** to **x** or changing **x** to **c** and adding -**es**.

> cactus –cacti
>   appendix – appendixes or appendices
>   nucleus – nuclei
>   index – indexes or indices

I. Irregular nouns with plural forms only.

> cactus –cacti
>   pajamas   jeans
>
>   pants   shorts

J. Irregular nouns that end in –s but are not plural.

> cactus –cacti
>   news   politics
>
>   athletics   rabies

Activity 1: Identify whether the noun is a regular plural (RP) or irregular plural (IP). Write RP or IP on the blanks.

____________ 1. hypotheses   ____________ 6. storms

____________ 2. volcanoes   ____________ 7. media

____________ 3. lice   ____________ 8. ponies

____________ 4. stimuli   ____________ 9. Physics

____________ 5. folios   ____________ 10. oxen

Activity 2: Write the plural forms of these irregular singular nouns.

1. syllabus - ____________   6. woman - ____________

2. basis - ____________   7. datum - ____________

3. bacterium - ____________   8. focus - ____________

4. mouse - ____________   9. thesis - ____________

5. tooth - ____________   10. fungus - ____________

Activity 3: Figure out the plural form of the word in the parenthesis. Write the correct plural noun on the blank to complete the sentence.

1. Mrs. De Leon has three ____________. (child)

2. I saw two ____________ in the kitchen last night. (mouse)

3. Grandpa is brushing his ____________. (tooth)

4. Those _______________ are making so much noise. (man)

5. I need to borrow your ___________. (scissors)

6. Many nations are experiencing multiple _____________. (crisis)

7. _________ thrive in dry and hot climate. (cactus)

8. Both of my ____________ hurt. (foot)

9. There are many _____________ outside the church. (person)

10.   I am afraid of many _______________ that cause illnesses. (bacterium)

Activity 4: Write a brief essay about your family. Underline the irregular nouns.

____

____

____

____

____

____

____

____

____

____

____

____

____

____

LESSON 3

Simple Tenses of Regular Verbs

Simple tense is the basic way to express an action. It tells when it happens. It is a verb tense for past, present, and future events.

The simple tense has no aspect that shows actions occurring at present, past, or future. It describes the action without stating whether it is ongoing or completed.

The three main simple tenses are Past, Present, and Future. Each tense is divided into Progressive, Perfect, and Progressive tenses.

To illustrate:

Simple Past   – I jumped.

Simple Present – I jump.

Simple Future   – I will jump.

Important things to remember about simple tenses:

- Past tense has a few patterns.
- Present tense uses the original form of the verb.
- Future tense requires *will* or *shall* before the verb.

Let's further explore the simple tenses.

Simple Past Tense

The **Simple Past Tense** describes the completed action that happened in the past. The action is completed for any duration (length of activity) or at any time (recent or distant past.)

How to form the simple past tense?

Regular verbs use:

- **ed** at the end to form affirmative action
- **didn't + verb** for negative
- **did + verb** for affirmative
- **didn't + subject for** negative interrogative

For example:

- His voice <u>echoed </u>in the room.
- He <u>lived </u>in America for 10 years.
- We didn't <u>walk</u> to the park.
- Did you <u>walk</u>?
- Didn't you <u>play</u> outside?

It is also associated with past time expressions.

1. Frequency – *always, sometimes, often*

    - I always <u>walked</u> home after work.

2. Indefinite point in time – a long time ago, the other week, ages ago

    - She <u>played</u> the guitar the other week.

3. Definite point in time – yesterday, when I was a child, three weeks ago

- I <u>finished </u>my task yesterday.

Simple Present Tense

The **Simple Present Tense** is a complex tense. It is used for actions happening now or in the present. It uses the verb **base form**. The third-person singular always has **–s** at the end (she plays, he sings.)

1. It is used to describe the habits (habitual actions) direction (or instruction), unchanging situations, general truths, and facts.

- I <u>love</u> cakes. (fact)
- I <u>watch</u> television at night. (habit)
- I <u>live</u> in Metro Manila. (unchanging situation)
- We <u>celebrate</u> Christmas in December. (general truth)
- Do not <u>play</u> outside. (direction/Instruction)

2. It is used to describe scheduled activities, fixed arrangement, or future events.

- The bus <u>arrives</u> at 8 o'clock.
- She <u>plays</u> with her brother on Sunday mornings.
- Her exam <u>starts</u> at 1 o'clock p.m.

3. It is used to tell stories, anecdotes, or jokes to make the readers/listeners more engaged.

- The skeleton <u>walks</u> into the room and <u>says</u> "Give me peanuts and pies."

Simple Future Tense

The **Simple Future Tense** is used to describe actions that will happen in the future. It expresses certainty or a fact. It refers to the time later than now.

It is also used to:

1. Predict a future event

   - I guess, it <u>will rain</u> tomorrow.

2. Express spontaneous decisions

   - I <u>will pay</u> the bills in cash.

3. Show willingness or unwillingness

   - He <u>will carry</u> your luggage.
   - I <u>will not/won't climb</u> the hill.

4. Ask instructions or advice

   - What <u>shall I do</u> to reach the hotel?

5. Make an offer or suggestion

   - <u>Shall I open</u> the door for you?
   - <u>Shall we dance?</u>

6. Give order or invitation
   - You <u>will stay</u> exactly where I want to.
   - <u>Will you marry</u> me?

Activity 1: Identify whether the following are in **Present**, **Past**, or **Future** tense.

____________ 1. will buy

____________ 2. eat

____________ 3. cleaned

____________ 4. formed

____________ 5. shall return

____________ 6. failed

____________ 7. will jump

____________ 8. washed

____________ 9. scream

____________ 10. will pack

Activity 2: Complete the following sentences with the correct verb tense.

1. We _________ the movie on Sunday. (watch, watched, will watch)

2. They ______ their grandparents last weekend. (visited, will visit, visit)

3. I ___________ our meal today. (cooks, cook, will cook)

4. She __________ swimming. (liked, will like, likes)

5. We ________ the song last year. (learns, learned, will learn)

6. I _______________ your book tomorrow. (borrowed, borrows, will borrow)

7. My sisters _____________ the marathon last year. (will run, ran, run)

8. He _____________ the letter to his father on Wednesday. (mailed, mail, will mail)

9. My mother _______________ the cake for my birthday today. (bakes, baked, will bake)

10.   I _____________ later. (will shower, showered, shower)

Activity 3: Fill in the missing verbs.

Past	Present	Future
loved		
	wash	
		will sing
	dance	
cleaned		
		will bake
shopped		
	jump	
fixed		
		will call

Activity 4: Use the following verbs in sentences. Show them in different tenses (Past, Present, and Future.)

work	want	count	call
paint	walk	look	
talk	smile	study	

1. ____

2. ____

3. ____

4. ____

5. ____

6. ____

7. ____

8. ____

9. ____

10. ____

LESSON 4

Aspects of Verbs

Aspects of verb describe the station of action of the verbs.

The four aspects of verbs:

- simple tenses
- progressive tenses
- perfect tenses
- perfect progressive tenses

Simple Past Tense and Progressive Tenses

```
Simple past tense      – I jumped.
Past progressive       – I was jumping.
Past perfect           – I had jumped.
Past perfect progressive – I had been jumping.
```

The **past progressive tense** of the verb talks about actions that happened over a period of time in the past. It requires the suffix "ing" after the base word.

The **past perfect tense** shows a completed activity or action in the past.

The **past perfect progressive** describes that the ongoing action or activity in the past is already finished.

Simple Present Tense and Progressive Tenses

Simple present tense   – I <u>jump</u>.
Present progressive   – I <u>am jumping.</u>
Present perfect   – I <u>have jumped</u>.
Present perfect progressive – I <u>have been jumping</u>.

The **present progressive tense** of the verb is used to show that something is not finished.

The **present perfect tense** is formed using the helping verbs "**has**" or "**have**" plus the past participle of the verb.

The **present perfect progressive** is used to show a continuous action that is now completed (recently) or an activity that began in the past and still going in the present.

Simple Future Tense and Progressive Tenses

Simple future tense   – I <u>will jump</u>.
Simple future progressive – I <u>will be jumping</u>.
Simple future perfect – I <u>will have finished</u>.
Simple future perfect progressive – I <u>will have been jumping</u>.

The **future progressive tense** of the verb is used to describe an ongoing event or action that will happen in the future.

The **future perfect tense** shows an action or activity or action that will be completed at some point in the future.

The **future perfect progressive** is used for an ongoing activity that will be finished at a specified period in the future.

Activity 1: Complete the following with the correct progressive tenses.

1. Simple past tense   –   I <u>danced</u> with my father.
   Past progressive   –   ____________
   Past perfect   –   ___________
   Past perfect progressive –   ___________

2. Simple present tense   –   I <u>study</u> nursing at the University of the Philippines.

   Present progressive   –   _______________________________
   Present perfect   –   _______________________________
   Present perfect progressive – _______________________________

3. Simple future tense   –   I <u>will graduate</u> this March.
   Simple future progressive –   ___________________________
   Simple future perfect –   ___________________________
   Simple future perfect progressive – _________________________

Activity 2: Identify the progressive aspect of the following verbs.

1. is creating - _____________________

2. was going - _____________________

3. will have hired   - _____________________

4. will have been climbing - _____________________

5. had walked - _____________________

6. have liked - _______________________

7. have been cooking - _______________________

8. will be visiting - _______________________

9. had worked - _______________________

10. will be planting - _______________________

Activity 3: Underline the verbs that are in progressive forms.

1. I was going to tell you the good news.
2. Our house has been sold to a friend.
3. The owners have decided to give us a bonus.
4. Our school principal is deciding whether to suspend the party.
5. The students have liked the decision to have a virtual event.
6. I can't believe that you had watched the movie without me.
7. She had doubled her effort to bring all the presents for children.
8. The company has been hiring more employees.
9. By the end of the day, I will have completed all my tasks.

10. I will have been travelling if there is no pandemic.

Activity 4: Write a brief essay about your goals and dreams in life. Use progressive verb forms.

____

____

____

____

____

____

____

____

____

LESSON 5

Prefixes, Suffixes, Roots, and Modals

Prefixes are words added to the beginning of the root words to give them a new meaning. They act as modifiers.

Suffixes are words added at the end of the root words to create a new meaning. They act as modifiers.

Roots are the basis of new words. They are part of the word that contains the core meaning, but cannot stand alone. Roots can be connected to prefixes, suffixes, and other roots to form new words.

The **Modals** are auxiliary verbs or helping verbs that add meaning to the main verbs. They express an obligation, possibility, permission, and ability.

Prefixes

Commonly-used prefixes and their meaning

Prefix	Meaning	Example
dis	opposite of, not	dis + satisfied = dissatisfied
mis	wrongly	mis + information = misinformation
re	again	re + read = reread
un	not	un + real = unreal
il	not	il + literate = illiterate
ir	no, not	ir + rational = irrational
im	not	im + mature = immature

in   into, without, not in + competent = incompetent

Suffixes

Commonly-used suffixes and their meaning

Suffix	Meaning	Example
-ness	denoting a state or condition	kind + ness = kindness
-age	act of, state of, result of, function, or collection of	pass + age = passage
-ity	degree, quality, state of	divine + ity = divinity
-ure	action, the resulting state	depart + ure = departure
-ment	the condition or state caused by the action	engage + ment = engagement
-ion	process, result, or state	decorate + ion = decoration
-hood	state of being	parent + hood =parenthood
-ends	denotes action	extends, suspends
-ence/ance	action or state	differ + ence = difference
		import + ance = importance
-ship	having a quality	member + ship = membership
-ism	a belief, condition	Hindu + ism = Hinduism

Roots

____

Commonly-used roots and their meaning

Roots	Meaning	Example
geo	earth	geography
bio	life	biography, biology
fer	carry	transfer
nom	name	nominate
chron	time	synchronize, chronology
tele	distant	telepathy, telegraph
ambi	both	ambiguous
aqua	water	aquarium
counter	against	encounter
fort	strength	fortress
mater	mother	maternity
mit	to send, to feel	resent, transmit
voc	to call, voice	advocate
dyna	power	dynamic
homo	same	homogenous
hetero	different	heteronym
micro	small	microbe

Modals

____

Commonly-used modals and their meaning

Modals	Meaning	Example
may	request permission	<u>May</u> I sit down, please?
	express possibility (present or future)	I <u>may</u> come home late.
might	express possibility (past, present, future)	He <u>might</u> have seen it already.
can	request permission	<u>Can</u> I open the door?
	express ability	I <u>can</u> speak French.
could	make a request	<u>Could</u> you say it again?
	give a suggestion	I <u>could</u> try to fix it.
be able to	express ability	I am <u>able to</u> pass the test.
shall	suggest, ask for help	<u>Shall</u> I do that for you?
should	give advice	You <u>should</u> stop eating.
	convey an idea or obligation	He <u>should</u> attend the meeting.

will	express intention	I will cook our breakfast.
	make a prediction	The day <u>will</u> be warm.
would	offer or request	<u>Would</u> you like a cup of coffee?
	in if-sentences	If I were you, I <u>would</u> walk.
Must/have to	express obligation	You <u>must</u> drink it now.
	express strong belief	She <u>must</u> be intelligent.

Activity 1: Add the correct prefix or suffix to complete the sentences.

1. She looks funny in her (dis, mis) _______ matched dress and shoes.

2. The (dis, mis) _______information campaign is going on.

3. My cousin is enjoying his single ______ (ship, hood).

4. His blind______ (hood, ness) makes him sad.

5. It is (il, ir) ______ legal to sell drugs.

6. The king ____(ship, ism) is a big responsibility.

7. Christian ______(ism, hood) is practised in different parts of the world.

8. Is the arrange_____ (ance, ment) acceptable to you?

9. The pupils need to (re, un) ______read the story.

10.   The (in, im) ____ consistency is causing the problem.

Activity 2: Use the following roots to create new words. The first one is already answered.

Roots	New Words
biblio	bibliography
cede	
circum	
ego	
equ	
hydro	
photo	
scope	
meter	
tele	

Activity 3: Pick the right modal to express a correct thought.

1. You _______ not be late again.
   - should
   - would

2. It ______ be done right now.
   - must
   - may

3. _____ you visit me tomorrow?
   - Can

- May

4. I _______ help you if you tell me what is wrong.
   - must
   - can

5. She ______ play the piano with excellence.
   - would
   - could

6. I will be ______ give you money this December.
   - able
   - can

7. She _______ see you next year when the pandemic is over.
   - have to
   - might

8. They _______ meet and discuss the next agenda.
   - have to
   - will

9. The teacher _______ announce the schedule of the next meeting.
   - can
   - shall

10.   You _______ tell your mother that you want a dog.
   - must
   - might

Activity 4: Write a two-paragraph essay describing your unforgettable experience. Include words with prefixes, suffixes, roots, and modals.

LESSON 6

Subject Pronouns and Indefinite Pronouns

Subject pronouns are pronouns that replace the nouns as a subject in the sentences or clauses. They perform the main action.

Indefinite pronouns do not refer to a particular person, amount, or thing. They can be singular or plural.

Subject Pronouns

	Singular	Plural
1st Person	I	We
2nd Person	You	You
3rd Person	He, She, It	It

Indefinite Pronouns

Singular	Singular	Plural	Singular or Plural
each much	anybody everybody nobody somebody	both few	all any
one	anyone everyone no one someone	several many	more most
either neither other	something anything everything	other	none some

another	nothing		

Pronoun Agreement

- The pronoun must agree with the words or word it replaces.

  If the antecedent (the word the pronoun refers to) is plural the pronoun must be plural. If it is singular, the pronoun should be singular.

  The pronoun and antecedents should also agree on the gender.

  For example:

  <u>She</u> agreed to give me <u>her</u> pen.
  <u>They</u> agreed to give me <u>their</u> pens.

Pronoun Reference

Unstated or weak reference

It happens when the subject pronoun does not have an antecedent to refer to.

- Lora is ambitious. **It** makes her work hard.
  (It refers to ambition. However, only the word ambitious is present in the sentence.)

- Jimmy left the group because he felt **they** impose extreme discipline. *(Who are **they**?)*

Ambiguous reference

It occurs when the readers cannot tell which antecedent is the subject that the pronoun refers to.

- When Nina put the flower vase on the table, it broke.
  (What broke? Is it the shelf or the flower vase?)

- Brenda told me that Mrs. Cruz did not remember **her**.
  (Are you referring to Brenda or Mrs. Cruz?)

General reference

The subject pronoun is used to refer to a general idea instead of a specific noun.

- The organization can no longer raise funds by selling tickets because **it** is now forbidden by the barangay regulation.
  (The pronoun does not refer to a particular idea.)

Activity 1: Choose the right <u>subject pronoun</u> to make the sentences complete.

1. __________ throws the ball so hard that her arms hurt.

   a. She
   b. They
   c. It

2. The cat stole away the cookie before _______ ran out of the door.

    a. she
    b. he
    c. it

3. _______ enjoy watching movies together.

    a. She
    b. We
    c. It

4. _______ is raining cats and dogs.

    a. They
    b. It
    c. We

5. _______ prefers to walk instead of taking a cab.

    a. He
    b. We
    c. It

Activity 2: Replace the following word or words with a pronoun.

1. Karen   - _________________

2. dad and mom - _________________

3. dog   - _________________

4. Jack   - _________________

5. Jill and I   - _________________

Activity 3: Underline the <u>indefinite pronouns</u> in the sentences.

1. (No one, someone) is knocking at the door now.

2. (Everything, Everybody) looked tired after the party.

3. (Anyone, Someone) can be a leader.

4. (Each, several) of us has a role to play.

5. (Something, Someone) should get the donations.

6. (Both, Each) of us can join the group.

7. (Everyone, Someone) is interested to attend the meeting.

8. (No one, Few) is coming today due to the heavy rain.

9. Please tell (someone, no one) to wash the fruits in the table.

10. (Everybody, Each) wants to win the jackpot prize.

Activity 4: Rewrite the following sentences to correct the pronoun reference issues.

- After Mrs. Gomez had scolded Andrew, she regretted her action.

  ____

- The literary program was not supported, which disappointed many students.

  ____

LESSON 7

Subject- Verb Agreement

The **subject-verb agreement** is important to effective writing and speaking.

The subject and the verb should always agree in number.

- If the subject is singular, the verb must be singular.
- If the subject is plural, the verb must be plural

Compound subjects have more than one noun or pronoun. They are joined by conjunctions. A compound subject can be plural or singular. They require a correct subject-verb agreement.

To illustrate subject-verb agreement:

Example 1: The <u>crowd</u> **is** asking for an encore.

Example 2: My <u>friends</u> **are** asking for an encore.

To illustrate compound subjects:

Example 1: Barry and Robin **like** coffee.

Example 2: Neither Barry nor Robin **likes** tea.

Example 3: Each girl and boy **receives** a gift.

- When the compound subject is doing similar action and joined by and, it needs a plural verb conjugation.

- When a compound subject has a singular and plural noun/pronoun and joined by "or" or "nor", it follows the rule of proximity. The verb agrees with the closer subject.

- When a compound subject is connected by and but preceded by "every", "each", or "no," the verb is singular.

Activity 1: Choose the write verb that agrees with the compound subject.

1. Cheese and macaroni ____________ (is, are) my favorite snack.

2. Neither my mother nor my father __________ (has, have) visited my uncle in France.

3. His wife and soulmate ____________ (makes, make) Oscar very happy.

4. Both Sherry and I ____________ (loves, love) watching classic movies.

5. Either my brother Eli or his best friend Carlo ______ (is, are) volunteering to clean the hall.

6. Ninoy Aquino and his wife, the former President Cory ______ (was, were) not afraid to speak their opinions.

7. The teachers and pupils ___________ (are, is) attending the symposium.

8. Neither Melissa nor Marissa _______ (is, are) going to the cinema.

9. Adult and children ___________ (have, has) something in common.

10. Adam and Billy ______ (were, was) deceived by the scammer.

Activity 2: Write the correct form of the verb to show the right subject-verb agreement.

Verb	Agrees with Compound Subject, Plural Subjects, You, and I	Agrees with Singular Subjects, He, She, and It
discuss	discuss	
need		needs
show		
love		
want		
study		
visit		
think		
choose		
encourage		

Activity 3: Combine each set of sentences to make a new sentence with a compound subject. Use the right form of the verb.

1. Ricky loves oranges. Diane loves grapes.

   ____

2. I like to eat pizza. My sister Becky loves to eat pizza.

   ____

3. Hot chocolate is on the menu. The pancake is on the menu.

    ____

4. The human heart is an important organ. The lungs are important organs.

    ____

5. Biology is an interesting subject. Chemistry is an interesting subject.

    ____

6. My sister loves to cook. My brothers love to cook, too.

    ____

7. Philip enjoys playing the guitar. Manny enjoys reading books.

    ____

8. I love bowling. My father loves badminton.

    ____

9. Exercise is good for the body. Sleep is good for the body.

    ____

10.   John is present on my birthday. Jenny is present on my birthday.

Activity 4: Share your thoughts about the ongoing pandemic due to Covid-19. Use compound subjects and correct form of verbs.

____
____
____
____
____
____
____
____
____

2nd QUARTER

LESSON 1

Order of Adjectives

Adjectives are words that describe or modify another person or object in the sentences.

Order of adjectives is observed when there is more than one adjective before the noun.

Generally, the order of adjectives is:

1. Quantity or number
2. Quality or opinion
3. Size
4. Age
5. Shape
6. Color
7. Proper adjective (nationality, other places of origin, material)
8. Purpose or qualifier

To illustrate the Order of Adjectives:

Determiner	Quantity or Number	Quality or Opinion	Size	Age	Shape	Color	Proper Adjective	Purpose of Qualifier	Noun
The	three	pretty	little			red	silk		hearts
A		nice		old		brown	Italian	sports	jacket
The	two				oval		French		rug

- **Quantity or Number**

  It answers the question "How many?" or "How much?" They refer to specific numbers (*5 or five*) or general amounts (*several, whole, or a lot.*)

- **Opinion or Quality**

  It expresses how you feel about something. (*pretty, beautiful, horrible*)

- **Size**

  It refers to descriptive size words like *big, little, large*, and more.

- **Age**

  Age-related adjectives include specific terms like 20-year-old or words like *old, young*, and so on.

- **Shape**

  It includes terms like *long, round, short*, or specific shapes like *circle, triangles*, and more.

- **Color**

  Color adjectives describe objects and animals. (*red, yellow, gray*)

- **Proper adjective** (nationality, other places of origin, material)

  It also includes religion and ethnicity. (*Christianity, Chinese, Filipino*)

  Material adjectives refer to the nouns that act as adjectives if they are used to describe other nouns. Examples are *silk, paper, metal*.

- **Purpose adjective**

  It describes specific objects. Purpose adjective is a noun used as an adjective.

ACTIVITIES

Activity 1: Identify the following adjectives. Write if it is quality, opinion, size, age, shape, color, origin/material, or qualifier/purpose.

1. green   - _______________

2. new   - _______________

3. Russian   - _______________

4. big   - _______________

5. antique   - _______________

6. square   - _______________

7. wonderful   - _______________

8. leather   - _______________

9. vintage   - _______________

10.   four   - _______________

Activity 2: Choose the correct order of adjectives for each sentence.

1. Our house is _______________.

   o large and green
   o green and large
   o large green

2. They buy _____________________ roses for their mother.

- o three, red, fresh
- o three, fresh, red
- o red, three, fresh

3. I like the ____________________ hand bag.

- o small, black, leather, stylish
- o black, stylish, leather, small
- o stylish, small, black, leather

4. My grandparents live in the _____________________ cottage near the beach.

- o Little, blue and yellow, French, beautiful
- o Blue and yellow, beautiful, French, little
- o Beautiful, little blue and yellow, French

5. I was happy to receive a ______________ puppy for my birthday.

- o Cute, 2-month-old, white, golden retriever
- o 2-month-old, golden retriever, cute, white
- o 2-month-old, cute, white, golden retriever

Activity 3: Circle the letter of the sentence that follows the correct order of adjectives.

1.
   a. I love wearing three, pretty, big, gold bracelets.
   b. I love wearing big, gold, pretty, three bracelets.
   c. I love wearing gold, three, pretty, big bracelets.

2.
  a. My parents bought a big, incredible, white house.
  b. My parents bought an incredible, big, white house.
  c. My parents bought a white, big, incredible house.

3.
  a. She receives a new, round, wooden table.
  b. She receives a wooden, round, new table.
  c. She receives a round, new, wooden table.

4.
  a. They have white, small, new, two boats.
  b. They have two, small, new, white boats.
  c. They have small, two, white, new boats.

5.
  a. I baked six pink delicious cupcakes.
  b. I baked delicious, six, pink cupcakes.
  c. I baked six, delicious, pink cupcakes.

Activity 4: Compose a short story about your pet using order of adjectives. Underline all the adjectives.

____
____
____
____
____
____
____
____
____

LESSON 2

Degrees of Regular and Irregular Adjectives

Degrees of adjectives refer to the comparison of two or more people, actions, things, and qualities in the sentence.

Regular adjectives have three degrees-

1. Positive Degree – makes no comparison
2. Comparative Degree –compares two people, actions, things, or qualities by adding –er or using more
3. Superlative Degree – compares the person, action, thing, or quality with the group by adding –est or using most

Irregular adjectives change completely to create comparative and superlative forms.

To illustrate Degrees of Regular Adjectives

Positive	Comparative	Superlative
long	longer	longest
tasty	tastier	tastiest
beautiful	more beautiful	most beautiful

To illustrate Degrees of Irregular Adjectives

Positive	Comparative	Superlative
little	less	least
bad	worse	worst
good	better	best

Activity 1: Write the missing degree of the **regular adjectives**.

Positive	Comparative	Superlative
old		
		shortest
	wiser	
careless		
	sadder	
		most famous
	prettier	
angry		
		gentlest
	more comfortable	

Activity 2: Write the missing degree of the **irregular adjectives**.

Positive	Comparative	Superlative
many		
		worst
	farther	
much		
		best
little		
well		

Activity 3: Complete the sentences by writing the correct degree of the adjectives.

1. This is the _______ hamburger I've ever tasted. (good)

2. Jasmin's voice is _______ than her sister Crystal. (beautiful)

3. I am _______ than my brother Peter. (old)

4. My cat is _________ (tiny) than my dog.

5. Santa Claus is _______ than my grandfather. (fat)

6. We visited the _________ farm in our town last year. (far)

7. I am a ______ piano player. (good)

8. They make the _________ donut. (bad)

9. Our farm produced the _____________ tomatoes. (better)

10.	Ken is _______________ than his twin Ben. (wonderful)

Activity 4: Compose a short story about you and your best friend. Use the three degrees of regular and irregular adjectives. Underline the adjectives.

____

____

____

____

____

____

____

____

____

LESSON 3

Adverbs of Intensity

Adverbs are words that are used to describe or change the meaning of a verb, an adjective, or another adverb.

Adverbs of intensity or intensifiers are adverbs used to express the intensity of the words that are being modified.

They amplify or downplay the meaning of the word.

Four Types of Adverbs of Intensity

1. **Emphasizers** – adverbs that help explain the ideas or feelings associated with the actions.

definitely	apparently	basically
really	certainly	literally

2. **Amplifiers** – adverbs that enhance or increase the intensity of the words they are modifying.

entirely	absolutely	remarkably
indisputably	extremely	totally

3. **Downtoners** – adverbs that downplay the intensity of adjectives, verb, and adverbs.

somewhat	nearly	merely
slightly	merely	sort of
	a little	

4. **Premodifiers** – adverbs that change the intensity of the modified words.

very	rather	relatively

Activity 1: Fill in the blanks with a correct adverb of intensity. Choose from the intensifiers in the box.

very	almost	calmly	extremely	rather
slightly	quite	totally	pretty	remarkably

1. I am _______ happy for your success.

2. The price of the guitar is _________ the same price of a mobile phone.

3. Are you _______ sure that she will like my gift?

4. I am __________ offended by your remarks.

5. Ben would ________ read a book instead of playing basketball.

6. We _______ agree with my mom's suggestion.

7. She __________ took the final exam and left without a word.

8. You did your task _____________.

9. It is __________ dangerous to go out nowadays.

10. It is _____________ obvious that you love cakes than pies.

Activity 2: Circle the word that does not belong to the group.

1.	extremely	very	snowy
2.	a little	much	quite
3.	somewhat	fairly	absolutely
4.	slightly	completely	entirely
5.	certainly	sort of	apparently

Activity 3: Use the following adverb of intensity in sentences.

<table>
<tr><td>almost</td><td>very</td><td>completely</td></tr>
<tr><td></td><td>quite</td><td>rather</td></tr>
</table>

1. ____

2. ____

3. ____

4. ____

5. ____

Activity 4: Write a short opinion about Covid-19 and how it is affecting the world.

____

____

____

____

____

____

____

____

____

LESSON 4

Adverbs of Frequency

Adverbs of frequency answer the question "How often?" or "How frequently?"

They describe how often action happens.

Adverbs of Definite Frequency

once, twice, thrice, four times

hourly, daily, weekly, monthly, annually

every minute, twice a month, once a year

The adverbs of definite frequency typically go in the **end** position.

- Most companies pay taxes <u>quarterly</u>.
- The board of directors meets <u>weekly</u> to review the status of the firm.
- Our team leader checks the progress of the task <u>every day</u>.

Adverbs of Indefinite Frequency

100% - always, constantly, usually, normally, regularly, often
        generally

50% - sometimes, rarely, seldom, infrequently, hardly ever
       occasionally

0% - never

The adverbs of indefinite frequency usually go in the **middle** position. They are **positioned before the main verb**, except the verb "to be."

For example:

- He is <u>always</u> late.
- I <u>usually</u> go to the mall every Sunday.
- She <u>seldom</u> watches horror movies.

Rules to observe:

> **Subject + adverb + main verb**

o Ben and Farah <u>often</u> go to lunch together.
o Marta <u>usually</u> goes to church on Sunday mornings.

> **Subject + to be + adverb**

o She **isn't** <u>normally</u> bad-tempered.
o My sister Becky, **is** <u>never</u> pleased when they call her Becka.

> **Subject + auxiliary + adverb + main verb**

o He **might** <u>never</u> see her again after their fight.
o I **would** <u>never</u> be unkind to someone who is need of my help.

> **Subject + adverb + used to/have to + main verb**

o We <u>usually</u> **have to** attend summer classes.

Often, usually, frequently, sometimes, and *occasionally* can go at the end or the beginning of the sentence.

- <u>Sometimes</u> my cousins visit and stay for a week.

- I play basketball <u>occasionally</u>.

Seldom and *rarely* can also be placed at the end of the sentence with the word *very*.

- John eats fish very **seldom**.

- They see their grandparents very **rarely**.

To form a question about frequency, "How often…?" is normally used. Another variation is to place the adverb of frequency before the verb.

- <u>How often</u> do you pray?

- <u>How often</u> does he go out to buy groceries?

- Do you <u>often</u> pray at night?

- Does he <u>often</u> go out to buy groceries?

ACTIVITIES

Activity 1: Rewrite the sentences using the suggested adverb of frequency. Make sure to place the adverb in the correct position.

1. My father reads the newspaper. (always)

   ____

2. Mrs. Vera Mall smiles. (never)

   ____

3. She drinks coffee. (sometimes)

   ____

4. I go to the park to watch people. (often)

   ____

5. She listens to rock music. (rarely)

   ____

6. My father reads the newspaper. (always)

   ____

7. They deliver the food. (monthly)

   ____

8. I check my email. (hourly)

____

9. I miss my best friend. (constantly)

____

10.   My uncle visits us. (twice a year)

____

Activity 2: Answer the following questions. Use the adverbs of frequency that are already present in the questions.

1. What do you **always** do on weekends?

____

2. Who do you **often** see after work?

____

3. Where do you **sometimes** go when you have extra time?

____

4. What show have you **never** watched on YouTube?

____

5. Why do you **rarely** attend parties?

____

Activity 3: Put the words in correct order to create sentences. Underline the adverbs of frequency.

1. late   never   pupils Her   are

   ____

2. I   at   finish   my   usually   job   5 o'clock

   ____

3. often   My   visits   on   grandmother   Sundays   us

   ____

4. occasionally   mother   takes   cinema   to   My   me   the

   ____

5. seldom   Steve   mall   the   goes   to

   ____

Activity 4: Write about your daily routine. Use appropriate adverbs of frequency.

____
____
____
____
____
____
____
____
____

LESSON 5

Adverbs of Manner

Adverbs of manner describe how something happens. They answer the question "how?"

They are normally placed after the subject or the main verb to modify their meaning.

Original sentence: She passed the examination.

With adverb of manner: She **easily** passed the examination.

Original sentence: He left the room.

With adverb of manner: He left the room **quickly**.

Activity 1: Choose the best adverb of manner to complete the sentences.

1. The driver of the taxi drives ______________.
   - recklessly
   - brightly
   - repeatedly

2. If you want to put on weight, eat ______________.
   - gently
   - healthily
   - lazily

3. I woke up late, so I need to shower ______________.
   - o hurriedly
   - o tenderly
   - o successfully

4. He waited ______________ for his brother to arrive.
   - o enormously
   - o constantly
   - o patiently

5. When you are in the library, speak ______________.
   - o quickly
   - o quietly
   - o cheerfully

6. My dog obeys my instructions ______________.
   - o angrily
   - o obediently
   - o irritably

7. Walk ______________ or you will miss the train.
   - o quickly
   - o slowly
   - o hungrily

8. The baby pounded the table ______________.
   - o personally
   - o variously
   - o excitedly

9. Playing music ______________ can damage your eardrum.
   - o loudly
   - o carelessly
   - o badly

10. The turtle walks ______________.
   ○ carefully
   ○ happily
   ○ slowly

Activity 2: Form adverbs of manner using the following words.

slow		terrible	
hungry		quick	
wonderful		innocent	
lucky		joyful	
calm		nice	

Activity 3: Complete the following sentences with the right adverbs of manner.

1. I speak English ______________.
2. She sings ______________.
3. I spend my money ______________.
4. He visits his friend ______________.
5. Bernard plays basketball ______________.
6. They ______________ beat the defending champion.
7. The girls talked ______________ about their favorite Korean actors.
8. Please answer my questions ______________.
9. I ______________ opened my eyes when I heard a loud crash.
10. I will win this board game ______________.

Activity 4: Compose a short essay about your most memorable Christmas celebration. Use adverbs of manner to highlight your experiences.

____

____

____

____

____

____

____

LESSON 6

Adverbs of Place and Time

Adverbs of place point out where the action is happening. They make the sentences clearer and more precise.

Adverbs of time indicate how often the action happens, when it happens, and for how long.

To illustrate the Adverbs of Place:

I stood quietly at the convenience store.

I stood quietly **inside** the convenience store.

____

- Adverbs of place talks about the location where things are happening.
  - here, there, inside, outside, indoors, outdoors, out, nearby, away, abroad, somewhere, upstairs

- They can be directional.
  - around
  - down
  - north
  - away
  - up

- They can indicate the object's position in relation to another object.
  - between
  - above
  - through
  - below
  - around

- Adverbs of place can refer to distances.
  - far away
  - nearby
  - miles apart

- They can indicate movement in specific directions. Many end with –ward or –wards.
  - forward
  - toward
  - backwards
  - westward
  - homeward
  - onwards

- Adverbs of place are typically placed after the main verb or object.

To illustrate Adverbs of Time:

Are you going to the movies **<u>later</u>**?

I am going to the bookstore **<u>tomorrow</u>**?

____

The most common single-word adverbs of time:

  - now, today, tomorrow, yesterday, then, tonight, this morning
  - already, yet, soon, later, before, lately, last year, never

____

- When placed at the end of the sentences, the adverb of time works best.

  - I am decluttering my stuff, so I am going to clean the house **today**.

- To show the exact number the action happens, place the adverb of time at the end of the sentence.

    o Our company has a spiritual retreat **annually**.

- To show how long the action happened, put the adverb of time at the end of the sentence.

    o I stayed at my mother's office **all day**.

- To emphasize certain aspects of the sentence, you can change the position of the adverbs of time.

    o Later, I will brush my teeth.
    o I will later brush my teeth.
    o I will brush my teeth later.

- Follow the following order when using two or more adverbs of time in the sentence.
    1. How long
    2. How often
    3. When

    o She went to Baguio City for **seven days every quarter last year**.

Activity 1: Use the suggested **adverbs of place** to complete the sentences.

> here   there   somewhere   everywhere   nowhere
>
> away   around   inside   up   down   outside

1. The salad bar is over _______, my dear.

2. I am looking _______ for you.

3. The yo-yo begins to spin ______ in the room.

4. I stood ______ and looked _________.

5. My father is ______ on a business trip.

6. Please stay with me for a while if you have ___________ else to go.

7. I believe I already met him ____________.

8. You can put the flowers _______ the table.

9. Come _______ the room and see my new dress.

10. They come here from ____________ to witness the grand celebration.

Activity 2: Choose the right **adverbs of time** to complete the sentences.

1. We cook Japanese food _______________.
   a. perfectly
   b. weekly
   c. normally

2. Have you completed your tasks ________?
   a. then
   b. yet
   c. still

3. I __________ want you to visit me every weekend.
   a. still
   b. then
   c. since

4. I haven't see you _______________ we graduated in high school.
   a. for a while
   b. just
   c. since

5. My cousin is living in France _____________.
   a. for a year
   b. not long
   c. ever

6. Starting _________ I will not eat junk foods.
   a. tomorrow
   b. then
   c. monthly

7. I will ask my coworker _______ to accompany in the cinema.
   a. yesterday
   b. today
   c. last month

8. I will see you _______.
   a. soon
   b. ever
   c. until then

9. He ______ writes a letter.
   a. daily
   b. occasionally
   c. now

10.   I ______ walk to school.
   a. often
   b. ages ago
   c. at the moment

Activity 3: Arrange the following adverbs of time properly.

1. a decade ago, for two months

   I visited New York _________________________.

2. five years ago, for eight months, every day

   I worked _____________________________________.

3. every month, last year, for two days

   He volunteered at the charity institution _________________________.

4. all day, for a week, last month

   My cousin and I played _____________________.

5. one day, a year ago, every month

   We used to see each other ________________________.

Activity 4: Write 5 sentences that show adverbs of time and adverbs of place.

1. ____

2. ____

3. ____

4. ____

5. ____

LESSON 7

Prepositions and Prepositional Phrases

Prepositions are words that link nouns, pronouns, and phrases to other words in sentences. They connect people, time, place, and objects to complete the thought.

They are typically placed in front of nouns and are usually short words.

Prepositional Phrases are groups of words that contain:

- a preposition
- a noun/pronoun object of the preposition
- modifier of the object
-

The preposition is pre-positioned before the object. They function as either adverb phrases or adjective phrases to modify other words in the sentence.

Types of Prepositions

1. Prepositions of time – indicate when something happens, happened, and will happen

before	after	at	in	on
about	throughout	during	until	

- For times of day, months, years, seasons, and centuries, use the preposition **in**
- For dates, days and specific holiday days, use **on**
- For times, festivals, and indicators of exception use **at**

2. Prepositions of place – indicate positions or locations

in	on	at	under	over
inside	outside		below	above

- **on** is used to refer something with a surface

- **in** is used to refer to something that is within or inside a confined boundary

- **at** is used to refer to something at a particular area or point

3. Prepositions of movement – describes how someone or something moves from one location to another

to	through	into	for	across
up	down	over	around	between

- **to** is commonly used to highlight the movement towards a particular point

- **into** refers to looking inside something or entering

- **across** indicates moving from one side to another

- **through** refers to moving directly inside and out the other end

- **around, past, down, up, over** indicate directions of movement.

4. Prepositions of manner

by   on   in   with   like

2 Kinds of Prepositional Phrases

1. <u>Adjectival phrases</u>– prepositional phrases that act upon the noun or behaving adjectivally

The dog **in the center** is the sweetest.

- The prepositional phrase "in the center" answers which is the sweetest dog.

We always buy groceries from Robinsons **on Pioneer Street.**

- "On Pioneer Street" provides information which store you are referring to.

I always wanted to live in a cottage **by the lake.**

- "By the lake" describes what kind of cabin you are dreaming of.

2. <u>Adverbial phrases</u>– prepositional phrases that modify or act upon verbs. They are behaving adverbially.

To know who get your cookie, look **behind you**.

He eats his meal **with gusto.**

- "Behind you" answers the question "look where?"

- "With gusto" answers the question "how?"

In rare cases, some nouns carry specific prepositions. They are known as dependent prepositions and act to consolidate their meanings.

Example:

He made another **attempt at** the championship round.

She has a wide **knowledge of** chemistry.

Activity 1: Circle all the prepositions below.

to	in	there	out
beside	behind	of	before
over	at	on	very
down	and	about	in
through	basically	absolutely	into
over	up	to	insect
he	we	on	across
when	where	between	behind
by	to	with	after
both	or	in	inside

Activity 2: Identify if the prepositional phrases are using a preposition of time, preposition of place, or preposition of movement.

1. on June 12, 1898   - _________________

2. on the wall   - _________________

3. to bed   - ________________

4. inside the car   - ________________

5. into the darkness   - ________________

6. at the entrance   - ________________

7. on the page   - ________________

8. on Monday   - ________________

9. during the holidays   - ________________

10. up the hill   - ________________

Activity 3: Underline the prepositional phrases in the sentences.

1. The flowers in the vase are peonies.

2. They are going to the convenience store.

3. My lunch break is after the English subject.

4. Are you walking on your tiptoes?

5. The bag with stripes is mine.

6. She walked up the stairs.

7. I looked under the sofa.

8. Please don't leave without your umbrella.

9. My mother made the scarf by hand.

10.　　He tried to finish the race at all cost.

Activity 4: Write a short essay about your town. Use different types of prepositions and prepositional phrases.

____

____

____

____

____

____

____

LESSON 8

Subordinate Conjunctions

Subordinating conjunctions or subordinate conjunctions are parts of speech that join independent (main sentence) to dependent (subordinate sentence.)

They perform two functions in the sentence:

1. Illustrates the importance of independent clauses or reduce the importance of one clause over the other

2. Provides a transition between two ideas in the sentence

(The transition indicates a time, place, or cause & effect relationship.)

Commonly-Used Subordinating Conjunctions

after	since	until
as	once	where
because	though	wherever
although	unless	when
before	so that	whenever
even if	rather than	whereas
even though	than	whether
if	provided that	why
in order to	that	while

There are 4 ways to make sentences using subordinate conjunctions:

1. <u>main clause + subordinate clause</u>

   I prefer to bake cookies and cakes **while** my son is at school.

2. <u>subordinate clause + main clause</u>

   Although Andrew assured me that he was fine, I still want to see him.

3. <u>main clause + essential relative clause</u>

   I edited the articles **that** were due tonight.

4. <u>main clause + nonessential relative clause</u>

   I sit on a couch to watch Spiderman, **which** is one of my favorite hero characters.

ACTIVITIES

Activity 1: Select the best answers to complete the following sentences.

1. _____________ the typhoon, people went out to see the extent of damage.

   a. Although
   b. After
   c. Before

2. I hired Laura, _________ her writing skill is fantastic.

a. after
b. if
c. because

3. They decided to stay at home ____________ go to the mall.

a. after
b. once
c. rather than

4. Every December 31 I stay awake ________ midnight to welcome the New Year.
a. although
b. until
c. though

5. Our dog barks loudly _____________ someone enters the room.

a. wherever
b. when
c. whenever

6. Patricia is reading ______________ her twin Pablo is writing.

a. while
b. provided that
c. as soon as

7. I don't want to attend the party ____________ I hate the noise.

a. because
b. so that
c. wherever

8. I am saving my allowance ___________ I could buy a new phone.

a. because
b. who
c. so that

9. He enjoys playing badminton ___________ he is not very good at it.

a. although
b. since
c. after

10.   The zoom meeting will start ________ the lunch break.

a. unless
b. if
c. after

Activity 2: Combine the sentences using the appropriate subordinating conjunctions.

while	after	since	because	until	even though

1. Mikka listens to her favorite song. She writes her novel.

   ____

2. He will not rest. He locates the missing book.

   ____

3. You are here. I will go out to buy some groceries.

   ____

4. I cannot accompany you today. My mother wants me to stay at home.

   ____

5. There is a lot to do. I want to go home.

   ____

Activity 3: Write complex sentences using the subordinating conjunctions in the list.

as	before	although	unless	if	once
after	so that	even though	as if	since	whenever
even if	though	till	because	whether	unless

1. She met her doctor. She finished her work. She is afraid.

   ____

   ____

2. My mother placed all my toys in a box. I can easily find my favorite toys. I want to play.

   ____

   ____

3. Tim's basketball team won the game. Two of their top players were injured. They showed good teamwork.

   ____

   ____

4. I will stay here. You are here. I want to be with you.

   ____

   ____

5. I do not eat junk foods anymore. I had a serious stomach ache. I miss my favorite chips.

____

____

Activity 4: Write 5 sentences using the given subordinating conjunction below.

1. provided that

____

2. in order to

____

3. unless

____

4. even though

____

5. so that

____

LESSON 9

Coordinate Conjunctions

Coordinating conjunction also known as coordinate conjunctions are words that join two or more words, sentences, main clauses, and other elements of the same syntactic importance or grammatical rank.

7 Coordinating Conjunctions

for   and   nor   but   or   yet   so

- and – joins two ideas

  I want to play volleyball **and** basketball.

- but –presents an opposing idea

  She wants broccoli **but** her mother gives her carrots.

- yet – shows a contrasting idea

  The cottage is simple **yet** so charming.

- or - shows an option or alternative

  It is so thick that I can scoop with using a spoon **or** a fork.

- nor – introduces a second negative idea

> Joy doesn't want to wash the dishes, **nor** does she finish her modules.

- for – explains a reason

> Our family eats vegetables regularly, **for** we want to be healthy.

- so – indicates a result or effect

> The coffee shop was closed, so I went home.

Activity 1: Combine the sentences. Use **for, and, but, or, yet, nor,** or **so**.

1. I don't want to be late. I wake up early.

   ____

2. Kitty has a lot of friends. She is a very nice girl.

   ____

3. I want to go to Disneyland. I want to go to Ocean Park.

4. Jim studied hard. He got a high grade.

   ____

5. She wants to go home. Her brother wants to go to the mall.

   ____

6. Our house is small. It is full of beautiful decors.

   ____

7. Do you like toasted bread? Do you like a sandwich?

   ____

8. Jeremy wants to be a lawyer. I enrolled in a law school.

   ____

9. I just finished packing my clothes. I forgot to put my favorite shirt.

   ____

10. We love camping. We love hiking.

   ____

Activity 2: Complete the following sentences with the correct coordinating conjunction.

for	and	nor	but	or	yet	so

1. I am going to be late, ___________ I will attend the meeting.

2. You pay using your debit card, ___________ you can pay with cash.

3. We live simply, ___________ full of love and harmony.

4. I was driving fast, ___________ I missed the right turn

5. I am going to be late, ___________ I will attend the meeting.

6. He doesn't like coffee, ___________ does he like tea.

7. She performed excellently, ___________ practiced a lot.

8. They are vegetarians, ___________ they do not eat meat.

9. He brought me a new dress, ___________ a new pair of shoes.

10. I want to lose weight, ___________ I find it hard to get a regular exercise.

Activity 3: Underline the conjunctions in the following sentences. Identify whether it is a **subordinating** or **coordinating** conjunction.

1. She cleaned the kitchen and the bedroom. _____________________

2. I washed my clothes while my sister took care of our little brother. _____________________

3. She wants a salad, but I want pasta. _____________________

4. I don't want to go outside, even though it is sunny.
   ____

5. The prince is so handsome, yet so humble.
   ____

6. I am going out, whether you like it or not. _______________________

7. Once they are here, give them your gifts. _______________________

8. We exercise every day, for we want to be fit.
   ____

9. Do you like a glass of milk or a cup of tea? _______________________

10. I love you because you are my brother.
    ____

Activity 4: Write a short essay relating the lessons you learned this 2020. Use coordinating conjunctions.

____

____

____

____

____

____

____

____

____

____

3rd QUARTER

LESSON 1

Kinds of Sentences for Specific Purpose & Audience

Asking Permission

Asking permission uses common modals can, could, may, would, do you mind.

Adding "please" when asking permission makes it sounds polite.

Structures of Asking Permission

> Can + subject + verb +?

Can you do it as soon as possible?

> Could subject + please + verb +?
>
> Do you think + subject could + verb +?

Could you please accompany me to the dentist?
Do you think we could borrow your guitar tomorrow?

May + subject + verb +?

May I go now?

Would you mind if + subject + verb in past +?

Would you mind if I he took his friend here?

Do you mind if + subject + verb simple present +?

Do you mind if I Leila takes you home?

Would you mind my/subject + verb + ing + your + object?

Would you mind my using your laptop for a while?
Would you mind Paul borrowing your favorite book?

Would it be possible for me + infinitive?

Would it be possible for me to travel without a medical clearance?

<u>Common answers when giving or denying permission</u>

A. Giving Permission

- o You have my permission
- o By all means
- o Certainly
- o It's okay with me
- o Sure go ahead
- o I won't stop you
- o No, I don't mind
- o Why not?

B. Denying Permission

- o You are not permitted to
- o You are not allowed to
- o I will not permit you to
- o No, you cannot
- o No, you may not
- o I absolutely forbid you
- o It is not allowed to
- o Yes, I do mind

ACTIVITIES

Activity 1: Use the following phrases to ask permission. Use the appropriate structure.

1. stay at home

   ____

2. watch a movie with a friend

   ____

3. borrow a dress

   ____

4. want to door closed

   ____

5. say something about the topic

   ____

6. left the meeting early

   ____

7. take pictures of someone's home

   ____

8. borrow P 500.00

____

9. have another cup of coffee

____

10.   ask an important question

____

Activity 2: Write your response to show permission.

1. Can I borrow your headphone for a while?

____

2. Would you mind if I open the window?

____

3. May we go out, please?

____

4. Would it be possible to cross the boundary now?

____

5. Could I have some dessert?

____

6. Can you help me finish my project?

____

7. Can I borrow your headphone for a while?

____

8. May I turn on the television?

____

9. Do you think I could get an approval from her tomorrow?

____

10.   Would you mind if I get more flowers?

____

LESSON 2

Kinds of Sentence for Specific Purpose & Audience
Responding to Questions

Interrogative sentence elicits information. It requires an answer.

Responding to questions depends on the type of the question.

<u>To illustrate</u>

- A Yes or No question

    Are you taking an online course?

- Polar question – subject-operator inversion

    He is reading a new book.

    Is he reading a new book?

- "Wh" or "Q" questions – requires a specific answer

    What are doing now?

    Where have you been?

    When is the opening of classes?

    Who are you?

    Why are you here?

How's your mother?

- Exclamatory question – displays emotional feelings, a type of a yes or no questions with an exclamation.

    Isn't she the most gorgeous person in the room?

    Aren't you the most fortunate girl to marry a prince?

- Tag question – short question that is added to a statement, eliciting a confirming answer from the audience

    He is not here, isn't he?

    The queen has arrived, hasn't she?

Activity 1: Answer the following questions.

1. What is special about this cake?

    ____

2. Who is having a concert?

    ____

3. She likes to dance, isn't she?

____

4. Do you sing?

____

5. When are you going to visit me?

____

6. Aren't we lucky to have a grand vacation before the pandemic?

____

7. What time did you wake up?

____

8. Why are you crying?

____

9. Was he affected by the news?

____

10.   You believe me, didn't you?

____

Activity 2: Form questions based on the following situations.

1. know the exact time the bus arrives

   ____

2. stroll at the beach

   ____

3. meet a friend

   ____

4. explanation about the report

   ____

5. the reason of her anger

   ____

6. reason why he didn't come

   ____

7. procedure to bake the moist cake

   ____

8. location of the gift shop

   ____

9. the price they pay for the tickets

   ____

10.   understand my instructions

____

LESSON 3

Kinds of Sentence for Specific Purpose & Audience

Making Request

Making request is about asking someone to do something for you or asking if you can do something.

Imperative sentences are used to express intentions or ask something.

To make a request, you need modal auxiliary verbs such as can, could, would, shall, or do you mind.

To illustrate:

Can you get me a glass of water, please?
Would you mind if I use your bathroom?
Shall I open the door for him?
Could I borrow money from you, please?

ACTIVITIES

Activity 1: Complete the sentences to make a request.

1. Can you _________________________________?

2. Shall we _________________________________?

3. Will you ________________________?

4. Could you ________________________?

5. Do you mind ________________________?

6. Would you mind ________________________?

7. Could I ________________________?

8. Can I ________________________?

9. Would you like me to ________________________?

10. Please, could you ________________________?

Activity 2: Make requests by using the following phrases:

1. a bottle of distilled water

____

2. leave a message for mother

____

3. reserve a seat

____

4. see another option

____

5. get a technical assistance

____

6. explain the reason

____

7. buy some milk

____

8. show me the pictures

____

9. the way to the supermarket

____

10.   have a room with a lake view

____

LESSON 4

Kinds of Sentence for Specific Purpose & Audience

Following & Giving Directions

The imperative sentence expresses a command or gives instruction and order.

It is used to give directions or follow specific instructions

- When giving directions, use short and basic English sentences. Speak slowly to help the person fully understand your instruction. If you are asking someone for directions, you can use "please" to be more polite.

- Use landmarks when giving directions or draw a map.

- Some words/phrases to use

  - next to
  - between
  - opposite
  - near
  - on the right or on the left
  - straight on
  - at the end
  - on the corner
  - in front of the
  - behind the
  - just around the

ACTIVITIES

Activity 1: Give instructions.

1. Excuse me! Could you please tell me the way to the café?

____

____

____

2. How can get I get from this corner to the MRT station?

____

____

____

3. Is the Starbucks next to the bookstore?

____

____

____

4. Can you help me please? Where is the shortest way to reach the Baker's Farm?

____

____

____

5. How can I reach the hotel?

____

____

____

6. Excuse me. Where is the bathroom?

____

____

____

7. Do you know where the bank is?

____

____

____

8. Can you please tell me the way to the principal's office?

____

____

____

9. I want to book a reservation. Please tell me how.

____

____

____

10. Would you mind telling me how to get to the post office?

____

____

____

Activity 2: Draw a simple map to help someone get from point A to point B. Add directions to help him reach the location.

LESSON 5

Kinds of Sentence for Specific Purpose & Audience

Expressing Opinions/Emotions

> Exclamatory sentences denote emotional feelings. Exclamative sentences are used to express strong opinions or emotions.
>
> Expressing feelings and opinions show your personal feelings and thoughts about something. They demonstrate how significant it is to you.

- Expressions that are commonly used to express opinions/emotions
  - in my experience
  - in my opinion
  - I really feel that
  - If you ask me
  - Personally, I think
  - I strongly believe that
  - What I mean is…
  - The point is
  - Some people say
  - According to the research

- Words that increase or decrease the intensity of emotions and opinions
  - Very
  - Extremely
  - So
  - Slightly
  - Fairly
  - Badly
  - Suddenly

Activity 1: Complete the following by expressing your emotion or opinion.

1. In my experience _______________________________________

   ____

2. I have no doubt that _______________________________________

   ____

3. It is often said that _______________________________________

   ____

4. I suppose that _______________________________________

   ____

5. I've heard that _______________________________________

   ____

6. As far as I am concerned _______________________________________

   ____

7. It seems to me that _______________________________________

   ____

8. To my mind _______________________________________

   ____

9. I bet that _______________________________________

   ____

10.   Apparently _______________________________________

   ____

Activity 2: Expressing an opinion or strong emotion. Write a brief, personal opinion about the following ideas.

1. Covid-19 pandemic

   ____

   ____

   ____

2. How to combat the climate change?

____

____

____

3. The best gift you received from your parents.

____

____

____

4. Role of internet

____

____

____

5. Online learning or classes

____

____

____

LESSON 6

Kinds of Sentence for Specific Purpose & Audience

Asserting

Declarative sentences convey subjective or objective ideas. They are used to express ideas, hope, wish as well as give information.

They come handy during language assertion to:

- describe your desire and feelings
- stand up for your personal rights and beliefs
- recognition of other feeling or situations and standing up for them
- describe what needs to be done
- describe a behavior
- express positive feeling
- acknowledging possibility of truth

To illustrate:

Excuse me, I would like to finish what I am saying.

We have the right to know what is going on.

I know there are rules, but I want these methods to be followed.

I declare my intention to run as Mayor next election.

I want to establish a clear boundary between us.

Let us uphold the civil rights that are embodied in our Constitution.

ACTIVITIES

Activity 1: Use the words/phrases to create asserting sentences.

1. freedom from hunger

   ____

2. independence

   ____

3. express your sympathy

   ____

4. point out your right to express your opinion

   ____

5. affirmation of support

   ____

6. rejecting the idea

   ____

7. recycling

   ____

8. smoking ban

____

9. prohibition of plastic bags

____

10.   pets' welfare

____

Activity 2: Compose a short essay that explain why you are supporting the implementation of curfew in your locality. Underline the asserting sentences you use.

____
____
____
____
____
____
____
____
____
____

4th QUARTER

LESSON 1

Compound Sentences

A compound sentence is a sentence with two or more independent clauses that are joined by a comma, semicolon, or coordinating conjunction.

An independent clause can stand alone. Joining two independent clauses make the sentence more interesting and meaningful.

Coordinating conjunctions for, and, nor, but, or, yet, so (FANBOYS) are used.

Another way to connect independent clauses is by using conjunctive adverbs (words or phrases) such as however, at least, moreover, and so on.

To illustrate:

comma + coordinating conjunction

Paris is in France, and Rome is in Italy.

I have known Emily for a long time, yet I never understood her.

independent clause + semicolon + independent clause

The sky is dark; it's going to rain today.

Tina studied hard; she topped the final examination.

semicolon + conjunctive adverb + comma

Mary likes Gary, however, Gary doesn't like Mary.

I love green salad, moreover, it is very healthy.

Activity 1: Complete the compound sentences by using a coordinating conjunction, conjunctive adverb, or semicolon.

otherwise	and	but	moreover
however	or	nor	yet

1. I like biking, _____________ it is a healthy form of exercise.

2. I would love to travel with you in London, __________ I need to renew my passport first.

3. The Mayon Volcano in Albay has a perfect cone ______ it looks majestic.

4. They turned over the donations to the Red Cross _____________ they would be distributing the items.

5. It is midnight, __________ they haven't arrived.

6. Beauty and the Beast is my favorite story, __________ I've only read it once so I cannot tell you the names of the other characters.

7. Should I ride the boat, _______ should I stay and wait for you here?

8. I only write fiction stories _______ I've never tried writing non-fiction.

9. There is no milk in the cupboard, _______ is there any eggs in the fridge.

10.   You can pay me online _____ I accept bank transfer.

Activity 2: Combine the pair of sentences to form compound sentences. Use semicolon, coordinating conjunction or conjunctive adverb.

1. I really need a long vacation. My job is very stressful.

   ____

2. I cannot blame him. He is innocent.

   ____

3. Her lower back pain is terrible. Mira refused to see a doctor.

   ____

4. We arrived early. We got the best seats.

   ____

5. The whole barangay was flooded. We used boats to rescue people.

____

6. She wants to lose weight. She eats chocolate every day.

____

7. The boys danced in the party. The girls sang.

____

8. I really need a long vacation. My job is very stressful.

____

9. I went to the department store. I only went window-shopping.

____

10.   Matt walked every morning. Jay rode his bike.

____

Activity 3: Complete the sentences below by adding a dependent clause.

1. She loves to watch cartoons, but _________________________________.

2. The bus was full, so _______________________________________.

3. Call me next Friday; _______________________________________.

4. I tried very hard to finish the project, however _____________________.

5. It is the perfect time to speak and _______________________________.

6. Mariah Carey is a fantastic singer; _______________________________.

7. I like the blue umbrella, yet _______________________________.

8. We are planning to go to Baguio or _______________________________.

9. My mother loves salad, moreover _______________________________.

10. I am going inside and _______________________________.

Activity 4: Compose a short essay about Christmas using simple and compound sentences. Circle the coordinating conjunction, semicolon, or conjunctive adverbs you use.

____

____

____

____

____

____

____

____

____

____

LESSON 2

Prefix de

Prefix **de-** means "from" or "off."

It also means away, down from, or from among.

It is used in different English words to indicate separation, removal, or privation.

Examples of words with de-:

- depend – hang from
- derive – to come from
- demote – to moved down from the current status
- detract – to drag from
- decide – to cut off poor options or false possibilities

Activity 1: List 10 words that begin with the prefix de-.

1.
2.
3.
4.
5.
6.
7.
8.

9.

10.

Activity 2: Use the words you listed above to create simple or compound sentences.

1. ____

2. ____

3. ____

4. ____

5. ____

6. ____

7. ____

8. ____

9. ____

10. ____

Activity 3: Fill in the blanks by writing the root word and the meaning of the new word. Number 1 is already answered.

prefix de- + root word = meaning of the word

1. decaffeinated - <u>de</u> + <u>caffeinated</u> = <u>not caffeinated</u>

2. deactivated - __ + __________ = __________

3. departed - __ + __________ = __________

4. decode - __ + __________ = __________

5. degenerate   - __   + __________   = ____________

6. degrade   - __   + __________   = ____________

7. defrost   - __   + __________   = ____________

8. dehydrated   - __   + __________   = ____________

9. dejoined   - __   + __________   = ____________

10.   Defuse   - __   + __________   = ____________

Activity 4: Write the opposite of the following words. Add the prefix de- to the root words.

1. recalibrate   - ____________________
2. recapitalize   - ____________________
3. reduplicate   - ____________________
4. reemphasize   - ____________________
5. reenergize   - ____________________
6. reforestation   - ____________________
7. refuel   - ____________________
8. reheat   - ____________________
9. reclassify   - ____________________

10. reload   - ____________________

LESSON 3

Complex Sentences

A complex sentence combines an independent clause with one or more dependent clauses.

The independent clauses express a complete thought, while dependent clauses (subordinating clauses) do not form a complete thought. They depend upon the independent clauses for meaning.

The dependent clauses always start with a relative pronoun or a subordinating conjunction.

The 5 basic relative pronouns are who, whom, whose, which, that.

The common subordinating conjunctions are because, although, once, since, whether, after, as, if, until, when, while and so on.

To illustrate:

Mobile phones have come a long way since *they were introduced on the market*.

<u>independent clause</u> + <u>subordinating conjunction</u> + <u>dependent clause</u>

For the first time, **I won the jackpot prize**.

dependent clause + independent clause

ACTIVITIES

Activity 1: Identify and underline the independent clauses in sentences.

1. Although I doubt his decision, I know that Dennis will try his best to complete the project.

2. Tina left in a hurry after he received a phone call.

3. They missed the MRT train because they were late.

4. I will leave soon, and I need to pack.

5. Even though I am younger, my brother Carlos is more independent.

6. I was quite upset because you are not here.

7. After this game, we are going to celebrate our victory.

8. I washed the dishes after I finished eating.

9. Because I was away, I missed the ending of my favorite telenovela.

10. She is not coming since I did not invite her.

Activity 2: Complete the complex sentences by adding an independent or dependent clause.

1. In the morning, _______________________________________.

2. _______________________ because we arrived early.

3. Unless you study hard, _________________________________.

4. Although I managed to escape, _________________________________.

5. _________________________________, I am now hungry.

6. Everybody laughed, _________________________________.

7. Although he is rich, _________________________________.

8. _________________________ once it gets cold.

9. _________________________ while her mom works in the corner.

10.   Whether you like it or not, _________________________________.

Activity 3: Tell whether the following is an independent clause or a dependent clause.

1. that Jim built   -   _________________________________

2. She played tennis   -   _________________________________

3. I had a good time   -   _________________________________

4. although she left early   -   _________________________________

5. but I will come with you -   _________________________________

6. If the barrier collapses   -   _________________________________

7. I like to see you now   -   _________________________________

8. He drove carefully   - _______________________________

9. Because it is Monday   - _______________________________

10.   Our new house is big - _______________________________

Activity 4: Write 1 simple sentence, 1 compound sentence, and 1 complex sentence.

____

____

____

____

____

____

LESSON 4

Suffixes –ary, -ate, -ee, and -eur

Suffixes **ary, ate, ee,** and **eur** have Latin origin. They primarily denote the agents or doer of something.

To illustrate:

Suffix	Meaning	Examples
ary	related to	honorary, missionary
ate	to cause	advocate, exonerate
ee	one who receives an action	employee, trustee
eur	one who	poseur, amateur

- Words ending in <u>suffix –ary</u> can be nouns, adjectives, or both.

  - nouns – *library, anniversary, secretary, beneficiary*
  - adjectives – *ordinary, extraordinary, stationary*
  - noun/adjective – *subsidiary, contemporary, complimentary*

- Words ending in <u>suffix–ate</u> form nouns, adjectives, or verbs from nouns and adjectives.

Forming nouns

  - Pertains to a chemical compound - *carbonate, stearate*

  - Refers to the product or result of a process- *condensate, filtrate*

- Denotes rank, office, or group with certain functions – *electorate, episcopate*

Forming adjectives

- possessing, having the characteristics or appearance of- *Latinate, fortunate, palmate*

- showing, full of – *passionate, considerate, literate*

- cause to become, act as – *regulate, activate, calibrate*

Forming verbs from nouns or adjectives

rusticate, hyphenate

- Words ending in <u>suffix –ee</u>

- denotes a person who is a beneficiary or object of the act specified by the transitive verb - *grantee, employee*

- indicates recent formation, mark the performer of the act, denotes the specified condition or state

  with intransitive verb as base *–returnee, escapee*
  with transitive verb as base   *–attendee*
  with another part of speech as base *–absentee, refugee*

- Words ending in <u>suffix –eur</u>

  - this French-derived suffix indicated one who does specified thing - *chauffeur, entrepreneur, monsieur, connoisseur*

Activity 1: Choose the correct suffix –ary, -ate, -ee-, or –eur.

Root Word	Suffix	Correct Word
rapport	eur	
abduct	ee	
pollen	ate	
discipline	ary	
donate	ee	
grand	eur	
value	ate	
compliment	art	
allot	ee	
regulation	ate	

Activity 2: List words ending in –ary and –ate.

-ary

1.

2.

3.

4.

5.

-ate

1.

2.

3.

4.

5.

Activity 3: List words ending in –ee and –eur.

-ee

1.

2.

3.

4.

5.

-eur

1.

2.

3.

4.

5.

Activity 4: Write the word that match the description of the description given below. The word should have a suffix –ary, -ate, -ee, or –eur.

1. not permanent _____________________ (ary)

2. recipient of an award ________________(ee)

3. to show appreciation _________________ (ate)

4. to make a copy ___________________ (ate)

5. a person working in a company ________________ (ee)

6. someone who attends ____________________(ee)

7. an expert _________________ (eur)

8. drives a car ________________(eur)

9. someone who is honored ________________(ary)

10.   one to whom a duty is assigned _______________ (ee)

LESSON 5

Compound-Complex Sentences

A **compound-complex sentence** combines a compound sentence and a complex sentence.

The compound sentence has two or more independent clauses.

The complex sentence has an independent clause with one or more dependent clauses.

Complex sentences have more parts than other types of sentences, helping the writers to express more complicated ideas.

To illustrate:

- Cathy doesn't like horror movies because they are scary, so she doesn't watch them.

  independent clause + independent clause + dependent clause

- While Jack reads, Sam prefers to eat because he is hungry.

  dependent clause + independent clause + independent clause

ACTIVITIES

Activity 1: Add the missing clause (independent or dependent) in the following compound-complex sentences.

1. Although I want to go swimming, I don't have time and
   _______________________________________.

2. I like to sleep but I need to get up early since
   _______________________.

3. If you have an extra time, _______________________________ and we will go to the mall.

4. _______________________________ after the sun sets, but today I prefer to stay home.

5. _______________________________, Chico knew he had to finish the game and he ran with determination to win.

6. The temperature suddenly dropped and it is cold outside,
   _______________________.

7. When the sky is clear, I like to walk around the neighborhood and
   _______________________________.

8. Elena loves her sister Elle, and Elle adores Elena because
   _______________________.

9. The rabbit ran off when he chased it,
   _______________________.

10. _______________________________ my friend wanted me to buy pizza, but I didn't have extra money.

Activity 2: Identify whether the sentence is compound complex, compound sentence, complex sentence, or simple sentence.

_____________________ 1. Timmy has a dog.

_____________________ 2. Kevin likes basketball, but Kyla likes volleyball.

_____________________ 3. The streets are flooded because it rained for two consecutive days.

_____________________4. Because I studied diligently, I received an A during our recitation, and I was so glad.

_____________________ 5. Since I have no milk in the fridge, I went out to buy in the nearest convenience store.

_____________________ 6. Alexa speaks Italian fluently, and she is going to teach me.

_____________________ 7. I am going to go my best friend's house.

_____________________ 8. Although he is poor, Eric tries hard to help other people, and he always give alms to the beggars.

_____________________ 9. I like latte but John likes cappuccino.

_____________________10. Do you know the woman who approached me earlier?

Activity 3: Make a compound-complex sentences by adding additional clauses to these simple sentences.

1. I swim every morning.

____

____

2. The classes start on Monday.

____

____

3. We live in Tagaytay City.

____

____

4. He likes to play baseball.

____

____

5. I swim every morning.

____

____

6. We meet every Sunday.

____

____

7. I swim every morning.

____

____

8. My dog barks a lot.

____

____

9. Mother makes a banana cake.

____

____

10.   They play football yesterday.

____

____

Activity 4: Do you have a favorite movie? Write a brief review about it. Use compound-complex sentences.

____

____

____

____